101
VALENTINE'S
DAY
JOKES
FOR KIDS

BLOOM BOOKS
FOR YOUNG READERS

Published by:
Bloom Books for Young Readers
an imprint of Ulysses Press
PO Box 3440
Berkeley, CA 94703

ISBN: 978-1-64604-613-3
Library of Congress Control Number: 2023943920

Printed in the United States by Versa Press
2 4 6 8 10 9 7 5 3 1

Image credits: cover hearts © kotoffei/Shutterstock .com; cover heart person © Zmiter; flying hearts © Evgeniya Mokeeva/Shutterstock.com; page border top © Tally189/Shutterstock.com. Cucumber and pickle cartoon created with the assistance of DALL-E.

What did the cucumber say to the pickle?

You mean a great dill to me.

What did the farmer give his wife for Valentine's Day?

Hogs and kisses.

Why is Thing so good at getting dates?

He's so HANDsome.

What kind of candy is never on time?

Choco-LATE.

Why was the rabbit happy?

Because somebunny loved him!

7

What did the muffin tell their valentine?

You're my stud-muffin!

Why do valentines have hearts on them?

Because brains would be pretty gross!

What did the ghost say to his girlfriend?

You look so boo-tiful!

What did one oar say to another?

Can I interest you in a little row-mance?

What did one sheep say to the other?

I love ewe!

And how did the other sheep respond?

You're not so baaaaaa-d yourself.

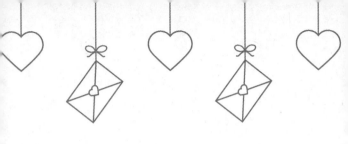

What do girl snakes write at the bottom of their letters?

With love and hisses.

What did the raspberry say to his valentine?

I love you berry much.

15

Why would you want to marry a goalie?

Because they're a real keeper!

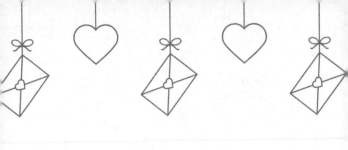

What did the dustpan say to the broom?

You sweep me off my feet!

What's the most romantic utensil?

A fork because it has valen-tines.

What are artichokes known for?

Their hearts.

What did one lightbulb say to the other on Valentine's Day?

I love you a watt.

What do you write in a slug's Valentine's Day card?

Be my valen-slime!

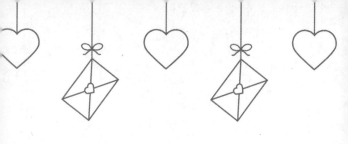

What did the cook say to his girlfriend?

You're bacon me crazy!

What did Frankenstein's monster say to his bride on Valentine's Day?

Be my valen-stein!

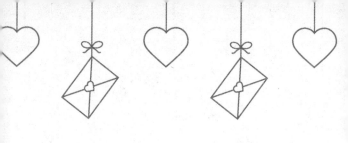

What was the thundercloud's favorite gift to give on Valentine's Day?

A box of shocklates.

What did the needle say to the thread?

You're sew special to me.

Why did the chicken cross the road?

Because her boyfriend was already on the other side.

Did Adam and Eve have a date?

No, they had an apple.

Where do bed bugs fall in love?

In the box spring.

What starts with a "p" and has thousands of letters in it on Valentine's Day?

The Post Office.

On Valentine's Day, what did the calculator say to the pencil?

You can count on me.

What's the most romantic ship?

CourtSHIP.

31

What did Robin Hood say to his girlfriend?

Sherwood like to be
your valentine.

What shade of red is your heart?

Beat red.

What do you get when you kiss a dragon on Valentine's Day?

Burned lips.

Have you got a date for Valentine's Day?

Yeah, it's February 14th.

What is the difference between a girl who is sick of her boyfriend and a sailor who falls into the ocean?

One is bored over a man, and the other is a man overboard.

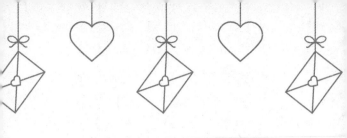

What did the shoe say to the lace on Valentine's Day?

You're my SOLEmate.

Why did the boy put candy under his pillow?

Because he wanted sweet dreams!

**And what did
the tweenager
give his mom?**

Ughs and kisses!

Why is Valentine's Day a good day for a party?

Because you can really party hearty!

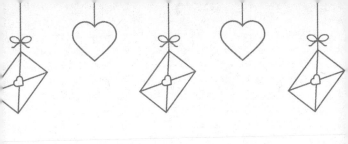

What did the scientist say to his sweetheart?

We've got good chemistry.

What's the best part about Valentine's Day?

The day after when all the candy is on sale.

What did the painter say to her sweetheart?

I love you with all my art.

Did you hear about the man who promised his girlfriend a diamond for Valentine's Day?

He took her to a baseball park.

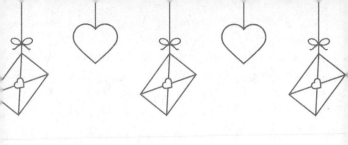

**Knock, knock.
Who's there?
Peas.
Peas who?**

Peas be my valentine!

What did the whale say to his sweetheart on Valentine's Day?

Whale you be mine?

What happens when you fall in love with a French chef?

You get buttered up.

What did the exit sign say to the door?

Wanna go out?

What did the paper clip say to the magnet?

I find you very attractive.

What did the chef give to their valentine?

A hug and a quiche!

**Knock, knock.
Who's there?
Howard.
Howard who?**

Howard you like to
be my valentine?

**Knock, knock.
Who's there?
Arthur.
Arthur who?**

**Arthur any chocolates
left for me?**

What Valentine's message was on the honeycomb?

Bee Mine.

How did the phone propose to his girlfriend?

He gave her a ring.

What did the baker say to his sweetheart?

I'm do-nuts about you!

What did the bunny say to her boyfriend?

You make me so hoppy!

What did one bee say to the other?

I love bee-ing with you, honey!

What did the tree say to the houseplant?

Do you beleaf in love?

Why don't you ever date a tennis player?

Because love means nothing to them.

What did the boy bat say to the girl bat on Valentine's Day?

You're fun to hang around with!

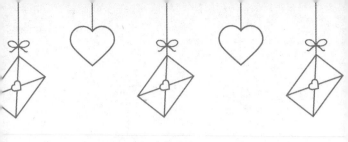

What did the stamp say to the envelope on Valentine's Day?

I'm stuck on you!

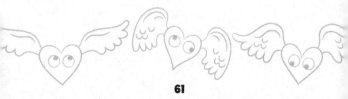

What type of shape is most popular on Valentine's Day?

Acute triangle.

What do you say to an octopus on Valentine's Day?

I want to hold your hand, hand, hand, hand, hand, hand, hand, hand!

What do you call a very small valentine?

A valen-tiny.

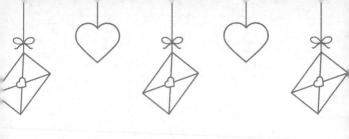

What did one watermelon seed say to the other on Valentine's Day?

You're one in a melon!

When do vampires fall in love?

At first bite.

What do ghosts say to one another to show that they care?

I love BOO!

What do you call two birds in love?

Tweethearts!

What did Facebook
say to TikTok?

My heart's all a Twitter.

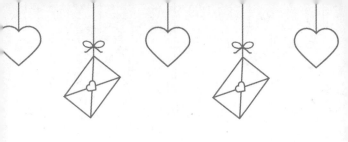

What did one Jedi say to the other on Valentine's Day?

Yoda one for me!

What do you call a ghost's true love?

Their ghoul-friend.

Did you hear about the nearsighted porcupine?

He fell in love with
a pin cushion!

Where did the hamburger take his date?

To the meatball.

What do you call the world's smallest Valentine's Day card?

A valen-teeny.

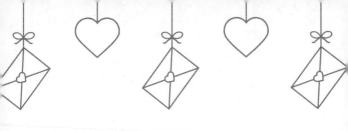

What flowers get the most kisses on Valentine's Day?

Tulips (two-lips).

What did one squirrel say to the other squirrel on Valentine's Day?

I'm nuts about you!

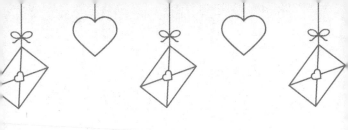

**Knock, knock.
Who's there?
Luke.
Luke who?**

Luke who got a valentine!

77

**Knock, knock.
Who's there?
Al.
Al who?**

**Al be your valentine
if you'll be mine.**

Why do skunks love Valentine's Day?

They are very scent-imental creatures.

What did ketchup say to the tomatoes?

I love you from my head to-ma-toes.

Why is lettuce so lovable?

It has a big heart.

Knock, knock.
Who's there?
Olive.
Olive who?

Olive you!!!

What do owls say to declare their love?

Owl be yours!

Why did the mango go out with the raisin?

She couldn't find a date.

Why did the rooster get a tattoo?

He wanted to impress the chicks!

**Knock, knock.
Who's there?
Frank.
Frank who?**

**Frank you for being
my friend!**

Why did everybody want to be banana's valentine?

He's so a-peeling.

What kind of flowers should you NOT give on Valentine's Day?

Cauliflowers!

What's the perfect thing to say to a coffee lover on Valentine's Day?

Words cannot espresso what you mean to me.

Why did the sheriff lock up her boyfriend?

He stole her heart.

Who always has a date on Valentine's Day?

A calendar.

Why didn't the skeleton want to send any Valentine's Day cards?

His heart wasn't in it.

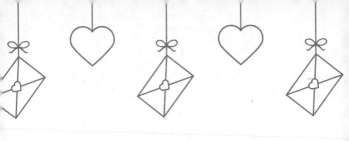

Knock, knock.
Who's there?
Atlas!
Atlas who?

Atlas, it's Valentine's Day!

What did the garlic knot say to the sauce on Valentine's Day?

You have a pizza my heart.

What is it called when fish fall in love?

Guppy love.

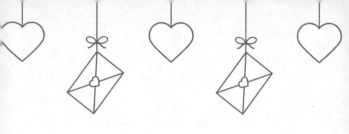

What did one volcano say to the other?

I lava you!

Knock, knock.
Who's there?
Bea.
Bea who?

Bea my valentine.

What did the butter say to the toast?

You're my butter half!

What did one piece of string say to another?

Be my valen-twine!

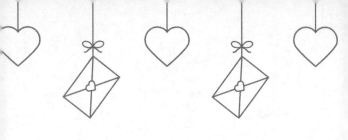

You should be in jail. . .

Because you just
stole my heart.

What did one cat say to the other cat on Valentine's Day?

Don't ever change, you're purrrfect.

Do you believe in love at first sight. . .

Or should I walk by again?

Do you like raisins?

How do you feel about a date?

Add Your Own Jokes!

_____

_____

_____

_____

_____

_____

_____

_____

_____

_____

_____

_____

_____